I0815510

ATLANTA HAWKS

BRENDAN FLYNN

WWW.APEXEDITIONS.COM

Copyright © 2026 by Apex Editions, Mendota Heights, MN 55120. All rights reserved. No part of this book may be reproduced or utilized in any form or by any means without written permission from the publisher. No part of this book may be used or reproduced in any manner for the purpose of training artificial intelligence technologies or systems.

Apex is distributed by North Star Editions:
sales@northstareditions.com | 888-417-0195

Produced for Apex by Red Line Editorial.

Photographs ©: Jayne Kamin-Oncea/AP Images, cover, 1; Tim Nwachukwu/Getty Images Sport/Getty Images, 4–5, 6–7; Bettmann/Getty Images, 8–9; Jack Zehrt/FPG/Archive Photos/Getty Images, 10–11; J. Walter Green/AP Images, 12–13; John Bazemore/AP Images, 14–15; Focus On Sport/Getty Images Sport/Getty Images, 16–17, 22–23, 24–25, 26–27, 29, 30–31; AP Images, 19; J. M. Hogan/AP Images, 20–21; Jonathan Daniel/Allsport/Getty Images Sport/Getty Images, 32–33; Kevin C. Cox/Getty Images Sport/Getty Images, 34–35, 36–37, 44–45, 52–53; Nell Redmond/AP Images, 39, 57; Don Frazier/AP Images, 40–41; Michael S. Green/AP Images, 42–43; Alex Goodlett/Getty Images Sport/Getty Images, 46–47; Bill Kostroun/AP Images, 48–49; Shutterstock Images, 50–51, 58–59; Maddie Meyer/Getty Images Sport/Getty Images, 54–55

Library of Congress Control Number: 2025945143

ISBN
979-8-89250-893-3 (hardcover)
979-8-89250-924-4 (paperback)
979-8-89824-000-4 (ebook pdf)
979-8-89250-955-8 (hosted ebook)

Printed in the United States of America
Mankato, MN
012026

NOTE TO PARENTS AND EDUCATORS

Apex books are designed to build literacy skills in striving readers. Exciting, high-interest content attracts and holds readers' attention. The text is carefully leveled to allow students to achieve success quickly.

TABLE OF CONTENTS

CHAPTER 1

TAKING DOWN THE SIXERS

The Atlanta Hawks are facing the Philadelphia 76ers. It's Game 7 of the 2021 conference semifinals. The 76ers had the best record in the Eastern Conference. But the Hawks aren't afraid.

Kevin Huerter scored a team-high 27 points against the Philadelphia 76ers in Game 7 of the 2021 conference semifinals.

The Hawks lead 90–87. Less than three minutes are left in the game. Then Atlanta's Trae Young comes up huge. The point guard puts up a shot from nearly 30 feet (9 m) away. The ball hits nothing but net. The Hawks hold on to win. They are headed to the conference finals.

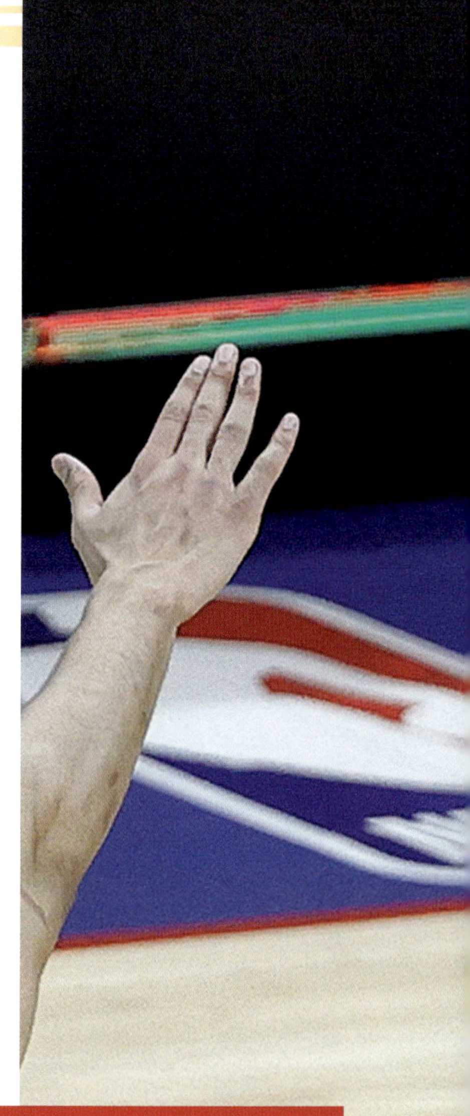

FLIPPING THE SCRIPT

In the 2020–21 regular season, the Hawks lost both games they played in Philadelphia, Pennsylvania. But the playoff series was a different story. The Hawks won three of four games on the road.

Trae Young shoots a three-pointer near the end of Game 7 of the 2021 conference semifinals.

CHAPTER 2

EARLY HISTORY

The Atlanta Hawks started in 1946. Back then, they were the Buffalo Bisons. But they soon moved to Illinois and became the Tri-Cities Blackhawks. In 1951, they moved to Milwaukee, Wisconsin. They shortened their name to the Hawks. After four seasons, the team moved to St. Louis, Missouri.

The St. Louis Hawks square off against the New York Knicks in a 1956 game.

St. Louis proved to be a great fit for the team. Star forward Bob Pettit led the Hawks on an incredible run. In their first season in St. Louis, they reached the playoffs. The next season, the Hawks reached the NBA Finals. But they fell to the Boston Celtics.

FORMING THE NBA

The Buffalo Bisons played in the National Basketball League (NBL). In 1949, the NBL joined together with another league. They formed the National Basketball Association (NBA).

Bob Pettit (9) takes a shot during a 1957 game against the Boston Celtics.

In 1958, the Hawks made it back to the Finals. They had a rematch against the Celtics. And they got their revenge. The Hawks beat Boston in six games. It was the team's first NBA title.

SECOND THOUGHTS?

The Hawks drafted center Bill Russell in 1956. They immediately traded him to the Boston Celtics. Russell became one of the greatest players ever. But the Hawks got Cliff Hagan and Ed Macauley in the deal. They helped beat Russell's Celtics for the 1958 championship.

Cliff Hagan (16) defends against the Boston Celtics in Game 2 of the 1958 NBA Finals.

The Hawks played their first four seasons in Atlanta at Georgia Tech's Alexander Memorial Coliseum.

The Hawks returned to the Finals in 1960 and 1961. But they lost both times. The team remained strong throughout the 1960s. However, owner Ben Kerner wanted a new arena. St. Louis wouldn't pay to build one. So, in 1968, Kerner sold the team to a group based in Georgia. The new owners moved the Hawks to Atlanta.

THE OMNI

Atlanta's Omni Coliseum opened in 1972. It was built for the Hawks and a new pro hockey team. The building was a success at first. But parts of it rusted quickly. It was torn down in 1997.

The Hawks began their time in Atlanta with five straight playoff appearances. However, they won just two playoff series in that time. That became a theme for the Hawks. They didn't have any trouble making the playoffs. But they had few deep postseason runs.

WILKINS DROPS 47

The Hawks faced the Celtics in the 1988 playoffs. The series went to Game 7. It became an instant classic. Hawks star Dominique Wilkins went toe to toe with Celtics legend Larry Bird. Wilkins scored 47 points. But the Celtics won 118–116.

Kevin Willis (42) was a key player for Atlanta during the mid-1980s and early 1990s.

PLAYER SPOTLIGHT

BOB PETTIT

Bob Pettit was one of the taller players of his era. He stood six feet, nine inches (206 cm). But he weighed just 205 pounds (93 kg) as a rookie in 1954. Some wondered whether his body would hold up against stronger players.

Pettit quickly put those doubts to rest. He earned the league's Rookie of the Year Award. Pettit played even better the next season. He won the first of his two Most Valuable Player (MVP) Awards. Pettit also came through for the Hawks in the 1958 Finals. He scored 50 points in Game 6. That lifted the Hawks to the championship.

BOB PETTIT AVERAGED AT LEAST 20 POINTS AND 12 REBOUNDS IN EACH OF HIS 11 NBA SEASONS.

HAWKS
9

CHAPTER 3

LEGENDS

Forward Cliff Hagan came to St. Louis in 1956. Center Ed Macauley did, too. Both lit up the scoreboard with their hook shots. They created a strong scoring trio with Bob Pettit.

Cliff Hagan takes a hook shot during Game 3 of the 1958 Finals.

Lou Hudson was a sweet-shooting guard. He spent 11 seasons with the Hawks. Hudson averaged 22 points per game during that time.

"Pistol" Pete Maravich was a magician on the court. He was famous for no-look passes and fancy dribbling.

BIG Z

Zelmo Beaty starred as the Hawks' starting center for much of the 1960s. He worked hard and played tough. Beaty averaged 17.4 points per game as a Hawk. He also grabbed 11.2 rebounds per game.

Lou Hudson made six straight All-Star Games with the Hawks.

In 1982–83, Tree Rollins led the NBA with 4.3 blocks per game.

Wayne “Tree” Rollins was seven feet, one inch (216 cm) tall. His nickname made perfect sense. Rollins towered like a tree trunk in the middle of the lane. And his arms extended like branches. Rollins became the team’s all-time leader in blocks.

REBOUNDING ROOKIE

John Drew was a good rebounder for his size. The small forward led the NBA in offensive rebounds in 1974–75. Drew was a rookie that season. He continued helping the team after that. He averaged more than 20 points per game as a Hawk.

Dan Roundfield played for the Hawks from 1978 to 1984. The forward was a strong rebounder. He made the All-Defensive Team five times. Roundfield could score, too. He averaged 17.6 points per game with the Hawks. Roundfield played a large role in the team's playoff runs.

GREAT DRAFT PICK

The Hawks drafted forward Kevin Willis in 1984. He became one of their top players. Willis earned All-Star honors in 1991–92. That season, he averaged 18.3 points and 15.5 rebounds per game.

Dan Roundfield made his third straight All-Star team in 1981–82.

PLAYER SPOTLIGHT

DOMINIQUE WILKINS

Few players excited Hawks fans more than Dominique Wilkins. The nine-time All-Star was an elite scorer. He averaged 26.4 points per game during his 12 years in Atlanta. Wilkins could shoot from the outside. He could slash to the hoop, too.

The high-flying Wilkins was also famous for his dunks. That's how he became known as the "Human Highlight Film." In 2015, the Hawks put a statue of Wilkins in front of their arena. It paid tribute to the Hall of Famer.

DOMINIQUE WILKINS WON THE NBA SLAM DUNK CONTEST IN 1985 AND 1990.

Gatorade

CHAPTER 4

RECENT HISTORY

Lenny Wilkens starred for the St. Louis Hawks in the 1960s. And he coached the Seattle SuperSonics to an NBA title in 1979. In 1993, the Hawks hired Wilkens to lead the team. The move turned out to be a great decision.

In Lenny Wilkens's first season coaching the Hawks, the team went 57–25. At the time, it was the best record in team history.

As a Hawk, Steve Smith averaged 19.9 points per game in the playoffs.

Wilkens led the Hawks to the playoffs six seasons in a row. But their postseason woes continued. During that streak, they never got past the second round. The Hawks went 28–54 in 1999–2000. That was Wilkens's final season in Atlanta. It was also the first of eight straight years without a playoff appearance.

BIG WINNER

During his time in Atlanta, Lenny Wilkens set the NBA career record for coaching wins. He also coached Team USA in 1996. The team won the Olympic gold medal that year. The games took place in Atlanta.

The Hawks snapped their postseason drought in 2008. That started a run of 10 straight playoff appearances. The highlight of that span came in 2014–15. Atlanta went 60–22 that season. The Hawks fought their way to the conference finals. However, they fell to the Cleveland Cavaliers.

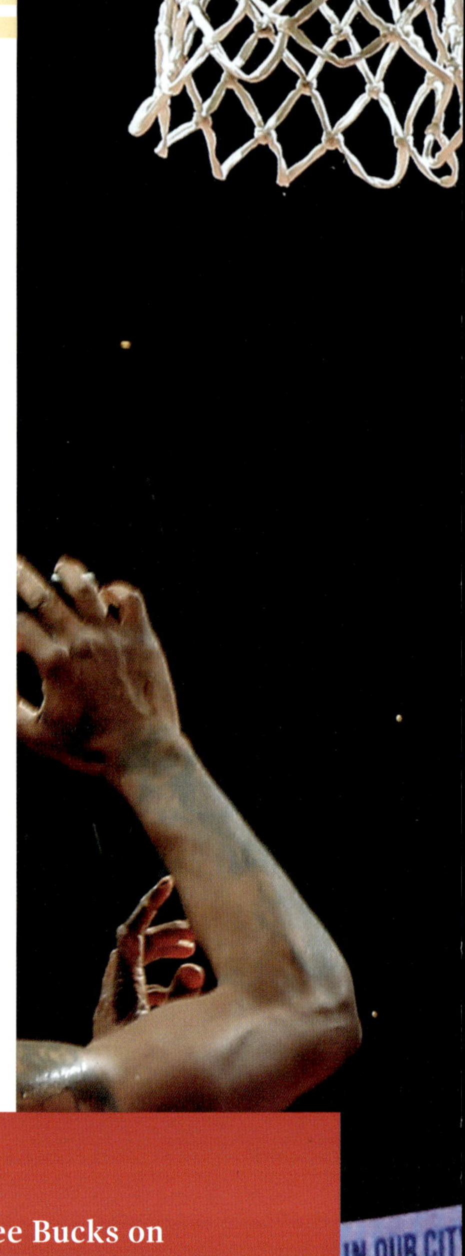

ON A ROLL

Atlanta beat the Milwaukee Bucks on December 27, 2014. It didn't seem like a big deal at the time. But the Hawks didn't lose again for more than a month. Their 19-game winning streak set a team record.

In 2014–15, six Atlanta players averaged at least 10 points per game. Al Horford was one, averaging 15.2.

Trae Young drives to the basket in a 2021 game.

The Hawks picked up rookie Trae Young in 2018. By 2021, the young superstar had led Atlanta back to the conference finals. The Hawks and the Bucks split the first two games. But in Game 3, Young sprained his ankle. Milwaukee won in six games. Even so, Young kept the Hawks competitive well into the 2020s.

CHANGE PAYS OFF

Going into March 2021, the Hawks were 14–20. Then they fired head coach Lloyd Pierce. The Hawks brought in Nate McMillan. He led a huge turnaround. Atlanta went 27–11 the rest of the way.

PLAYER SPOTLIGHT

TRAE YOUNG

Trae Young quickly became the Hawks' team leader in 2018. He dropped 35 points in his third NBA game. He recorded 11 assists in that game, too. Young also became known for his clutch play. For example, he opened the 2021 conference finals with an amazing game. He scored 48 points. He dished out 11 assists. And he grabbed seven rebounds.

Young's game continued to develop. He grew into an elite playmaker. In 2024–25, he averaged 11.6 assists per game. That led the NBA. It was no surprise that Young made his fourth All-Star team that season.

TRAE YOUNG AVERAGED 25.3 POINTS PER GAME IN HIS FIRST SEVEN SEASONS.

ATLANTA
11

CHAPTER 5

MODERN STARS

Dikembe Mutombo towered over opponents. He stood seven feet, two inches (218 cm) tall. Mutombo was one of the greatest shot blockers in NBA history. He won the Defensive Player of the Year Award three times as a Hawk.

Dikembe Mutombo denies an Orlando Magic player during a 2000 game.

Mookie Blaylock played alongside Mutombo. Together, they turned the Hawks into a defensive powerhouse. Blaylock was just six feet (183 cm) tall. But the point guard had lightning-quick hands. He led the NBA in steals two seasons in a row.

SCORING BOOST

In 1994, the Hawks needed scoring. So, they traded for Steve Smith. The guard came through for Atlanta. He averaged 18.6 points per game over the next five seasons.

Mookie Blaylock made the All-Defensive Team six times in his career.

Joe Johnson was a silky shooter. The veteran guard came to the Hawks in 2005. That's when his career took off. In 2005–06, Johnson averaged 20 points per game for the first time. He made the All-Star team the next six seasons.

STAR CENTER

In college, center Al Horford led Florida to two national titles. Then the Hawks drafted him in 2007. Horford spent nine seasons with the Hawks. He made the All-Star Game four times.

Joe Johnson averaged 20.9 points per game over seven seasons with the Hawks.

Power forward Paul Millsap spent only four seasons in Atlanta. But he was an All-Star in each one. Millsap also helped the Hawks reach the 2015 conference finals. He led the team in scoring that season.

REBOUNDING CHAMPION

Center Clint Capela arrived in Atlanta in 2020. That season, he grabbed 14.3 rebounds per game. That led the league. Capela also averaged 15.2 points and 2.0 blocks. He helped the Hawks return to the conference finals.

Paul Millsap averaged 17.4 points and 8.3 rebounds with the Hawks.

CHAPTER 6

TEAM TRIVIA

The Hawks' team colors have changed a lot over the years. Red and gold have often been their main colors. But they've worn other colors, too. For example, from 1970 to 1972, they went with royal blue and light green.

From 2007 to 2015, the Hawks wore navy blue and red.

The Hawks' arena can host more than 17,000 fans.

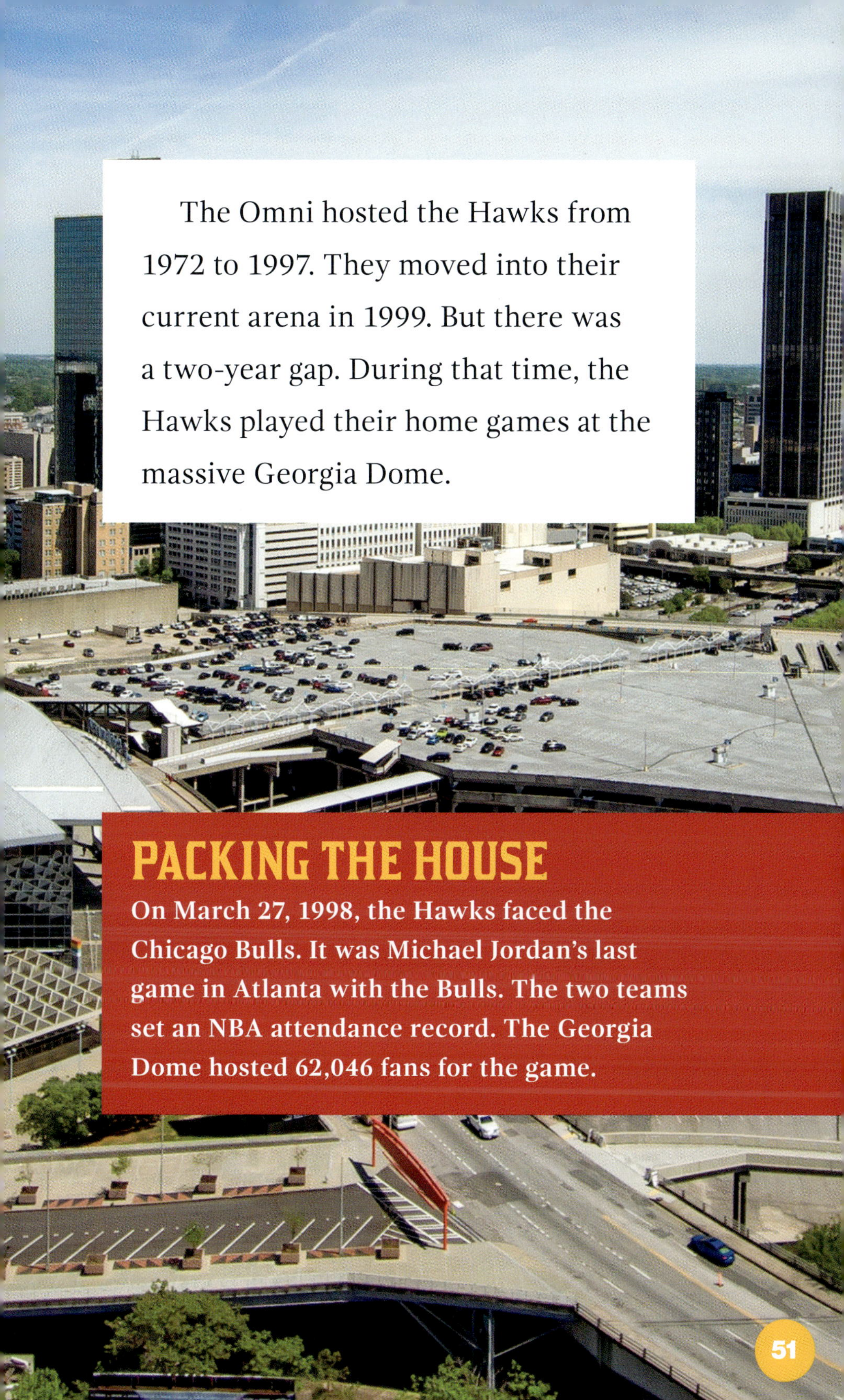

The Omni hosted the Hawks from 1972 to 1997. They moved into their current arena in 1999. But there was a two-year gap. During that time, the Hawks played their home games at the massive Georgia Dome.

PACKING THE HOUSE

On March 27, 1998, the Hawks faced the Chicago Bulls. It was Michael Jordan's last game in Atlanta with the Bulls. The two teams set an NBA attendance record. The Georgia Dome hosted 62,046 fans for the game.

Harry the Hawk soars through the air for a dunk at a 2015 game.

Harry the Hawk was "hatched" in 1986. He became Atlanta's mascot. Harry is known for his incredible dance moves. He also thrills fans with his dunks and sideline antics.

SHORTEST SLAM DUNK CHAMP

Anthony "Spud" Webb played for the Hawks from 1985 to 1991 and in 1995–96. He was a fan favorite. In a league of giants, Webb stood only five feet, six inches (168 cm) tall. In 1986, he became the shortest player to win the NBA Slam Dunk Contest.

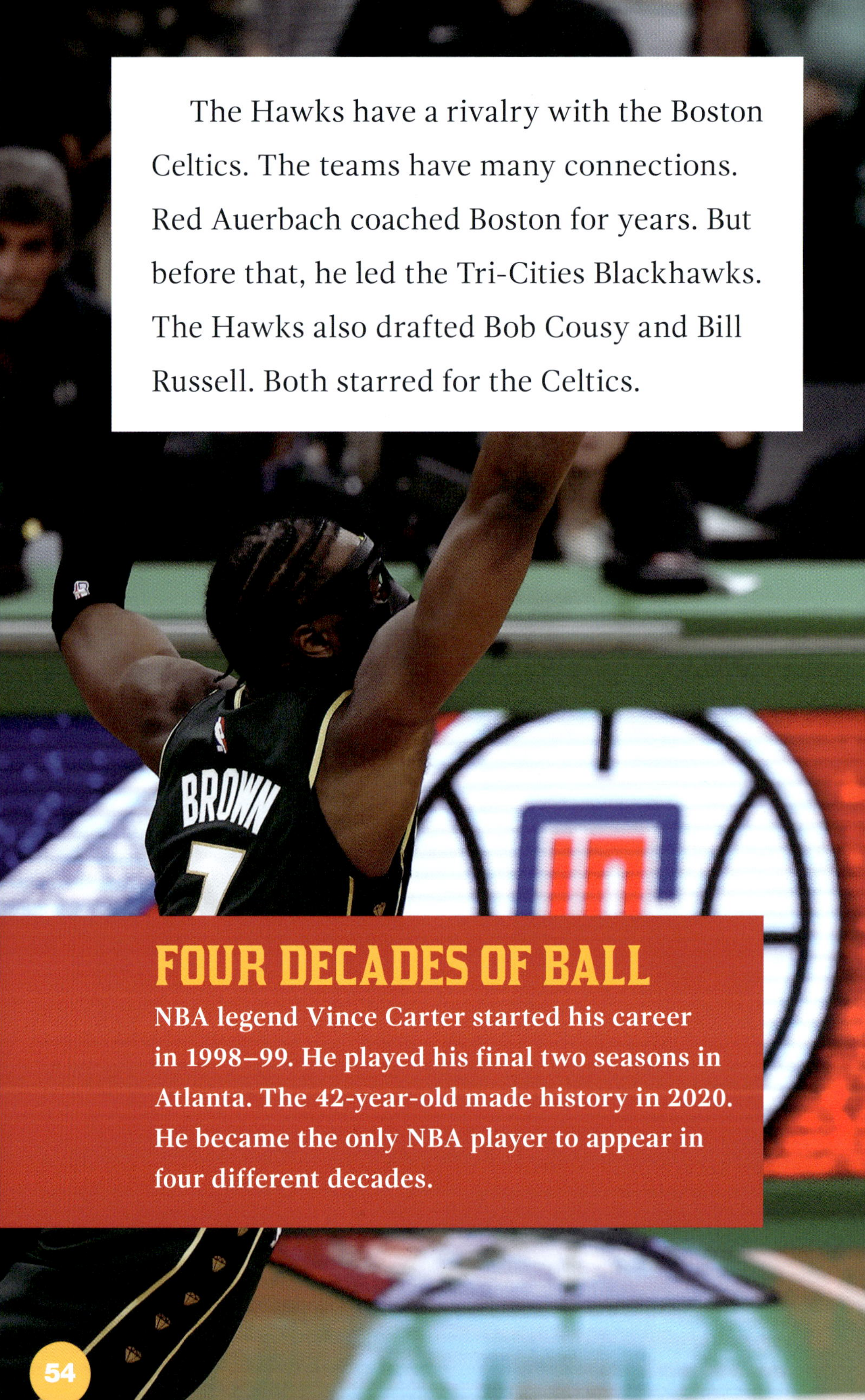

The Hawks have a rivalry with the Boston Celtics. The teams have many connections. Red Auerbach coached Boston for years. But before that, he led the Tri-Cities Blackhawks. The Hawks also drafted Bob Cousy and Bill Russell. Both starred for the Celtics.

FOUR DECADES OF BALL

NBA legend Vince Carter started his career in 1998–99. He played his final two seasons in Atlanta. The 42-year-old made history in 2020. He became the only NBA player to appear in four different decades.

Trae Young sinks a game-winner during the 2023 playoffs against the Celtics.

TEAM RECORDS

All-Time Points: 23,292
Dominique Wilkins (1982–94)

All-Time Assists: 4,748
Trae Young (2018–)

All-Time Rebounds: 12,849
Bob Pettit (1954–65)

All-Time Steals: 1,321
Mookie Blaylock (1992–99)

All-Time Blocks: 2,283
Tree Rollins (1977–88)

All-Time Three-Pointers: 1,277
Trae Young (2018–)

All-Time Triple-Doubles: 7
Mookie Blaylock (1992–99)

All-Time Coaching Wins: 327
Richie Guerin (1964–72)

NBA MVPs: 2
Bob Pettit (1955–56, 1958–59)

NBA Championships: 1
1957–58

All statistics are accurate through the 2024–25 season.

ATLANTA
11

TIMELINE

1946

The Buffalo Bisons of the NBL move to Illinois and become the Tri-Cities Blackhawks.

1951

The team moves to Wisconsin and changes its name to the Milwaukee Hawks.

1955

The Hawks move again, this time to St. Louis, Missouri.

1958

Hall of Famer Bob Pettit leads the Hawks to their first NBA title.

1968

The Hawks are sold and move to Atlanta, Georgia.

1985

1993

2015

2021

2025

Dominique Wilkins wins the first of his two Slam Dunk titles.

Former Hawks star Lenny Wilkens is hired as head coach.

After winning 19 straight games in the regular season, the Hawks reach the conference finals, where they fall to the Cleveland Cavaliers.

The Hawks return to the conference finals but lose to the Milwaukee Bucks in six games.

Trae Young leads the NBA with 11.6 assists per game.

COMPREHENSION QUESTIONS

Write your answers on a separate piece of paper.

1. Write a paragraph that explains the main ideas of Chapter 4.
2. Who do you think was the greatest player in Hawks history? Why?
3. Why did the Hawks move to Atlanta in 1968?
   - A. Their star player forced them to move.
   - B. They were sold to a group from Georgia.
   - C. Their owner helped form a new league.
4. Why were people surprised to see Spud Webb win the Slam Dunk Contest?
   - A. Webb was very short for an NBA player.
   - B. Webb was playing with an injured leg.
   - C. Webb hadn't dunked before in a game.

5. What does **tribute** mean in this book?

In 2015, the Hawks put a statue of Wilkins in front of their arena. It paid ***tribute*** *to the Hall of Famer.*

A. respect
B. similarity
C. fame

6. What does **woes** mean in this book?

But their postseason ***woes*** *continued. During that streak, they never got past the second round.*

A. games
B. problems
C. success

Answer key on page 64.

GLOSSARY

assists
Passes that lead directly to baskets.

center
A tall player who usually plays near the hoop.

clutch
Having to do with a difficult situation when the outcome of the game is in question.

conference
A group of teams that make up part of a sports league.

drafted
Selected a new player coming into the league.

drought
A long time without success.

elite
The best of the best.

playoff
A set of games played after the regular season to decide which team is the champion.

rivalry
An ongoing competition that brings out strong emotion from fans and players.

rookie
An athlete in his or her first year as a professional player.

veteran
A person who has been doing his or her job for a long time.

TO LEARN MORE

BOOKS

Coleman, Ted. *Atlanta Hawks All-Time Greats.* Press Box Books, 2023.

Grack, Rachel A. *Everything NBA.* Bellwether Media, 2026.

Hewson, Anthony K. *Atlanta Hawks.* Abdo Publishing, 2023.

ONLINE RESOURCES

Visit **www.apexeditions.com** to find links and resources related to this title.

ABOUT THE AUTHOR

Brendan Flynn lives in Minneapolis, Minnesota. In addition to writing about sports, Flynn enjoys solving crossword puzzles, trying new recipes in the kitchen, and walking around the beautiful lakes of Minneapolis.

INDEX

ANSWER KEY:

1. Answers will vary; 2. Answers will vary; 3. B; 4. A; 5. A; 6. B